baby massage

**Anita Epple and
Pauline Carpenter**

For UK order enquiries: please contact Bookpoint Ltd, 130 Milton Park, Abingdon, Oxon OX14 4SB. *Telephone*: +44 (0) 1235 827720. *Fax*: +44 (0) 1235 400454. Lines are open 09.00–17.00, Monday to Saturday, with a 24-hour message answering service. Details about our titles and how to order are available at www.hoddereducation.com

British Library Cataloguing in Publication Data: a catalogue record for this title is available from the British Library.

First published in UK 2011 by Hodder Education, part of Hachette UK, 338 Euston Road, London NW1 3BH.

Typeset by MPS Limited, a Macmillan Company.

Printed in Great Britain for Hodder Education, an Hachette UK Company, 338 Euston Road, London NW1 3BH, by CPI Cox & Wyman, Reading, Berkshire RG1 8EX.

The publisher has used its best endeavours to ensure that the URLs for external websites referred to in this book are correct and active at the time of going to press. However, the publisher and the author have no responsibility for the websites and can make no guarantee that a site will remain live or that the content will remain relevant, decent or appropriate.

Hachette UK's policy is to use papers that are natural, renewable and recyclable products and made from wood grown in sustainable forests. The logging and manufacturing processes are expected to conform to the environmental regulations of the country of origin.

Impression number   10 9 8 7 6 5 4 3 2 1

Year   2015 2014 2013 2012 2011

To our children Kristi, Tim, Lucy, Anna, Manon and Amélie for whom loving touch is a part of their everyday lives.

Contents

introduction

Baby Massage is a quick and easy-to-follow guide for parents who would like to discover more about the wonderful art of massage with their babies.

In the following pages, you will find a full body massage routine for baby, explained in simple step-by-step instructions, accompanied by clear illustrations that guide you reassuringly through the whole massage. In addition there is useful information to ensure that this special pleasure can be carried out safely in the comfort of your home:

* when is the best time to do massage with your baby
* the best oils to use
* the importance of being comfortable during the routine.

The routine is divided into bite-sized sections to build confidence, whilst giving your baby a gentle introduction to massage.

Baby massage is a remarkable skill to learn, not only because there are a host of physical benefits but also because it helps to build a life-long relationship between you and your baby.

Why massage is good for your baby and you

Emotional benefits

When the subject of baby massage is discussed, it is often the physical benefits that are considered first, but there are also a number of emotional benefits to be gained by both the baby and the parent when they engage in baby massage on a regular basis.

Helping your baby adapt to their new environment

Upon leaving the comfort of their mother's womb, a newborn can find that entering the new phase of their life is rather stressful. Massage, however, can reduce stress, which is as important for tiny babies as it is for adults! Regular massage can help babies adapt to their new environment and reassure them. In time, when they feel anxious, out of sorts or in a stressful situation, parents can use massage, which their baby recognizes as a pleasant experience, to help calm and soothe their baby.

Overcoming intrusive medical intervention

Massage can help babies that have received intrusive medical interventions and may associate touch with a negative experience. If your baby has received some medical intervention, you might find initially that massage may be far too stimulating and distressing for your baby, but you can overcome this by gently introducing the concept of positive touch to them. This can simply be stroking over your baby's clothes, while holding them securely and talking to them soothingly.

Gradually you will be able to progress to the massage routine (see Chapters 5–10), being guided by your baby's subtle forms of communication (see 'Understanding what your baby is telling you' in Chapter 2).

Understanding your baby

Through massage you can learn how your baby communicates with you by understanding their positive and negative cues (see Chapter 2). These are the noises, movements and subtle physical changes that your baby makes. This may help you to feel more in control as you gain a greater understanding of your baby and you will find that this enhances the mutual respect between you.

Bonding with your baby

Touch, eye contact, smell and sounds of the parent's voice are all elements of the bonding process between parent and baby. However, because of the pressures to return to work soon after birth, there is a need for parents and babies to become less dependent upon each other very quickly. Spending time holding, touching and chatting to our babies happens less frequently and because of this the bonding process may be affected.

Sibling rivalry

When a new baby arrives into a family that already has one or more children, the family dynamics can be changed dramatically. Older siblings can feel alienated, neglected and just down-right jealous of the new arrival. Parents who are sensitive to this know the importance of helping the older children come to terms with and accept the new baby. Baby massage can be extremely useful in this process.

If you have older children, you can really help make a difference to the way they feel about your new baby by involving them in the routines, such as preparing the room, thereby showing them that they are still just as important to you as they always were. Not only that, they may enjoy the new found responsibility as 'older' brother or sister.

Physical benefits

Strengthens body systems

Regular massage may help to strengthen your baby's immune system and increase their resistance to infection. It may also improve blood circulation and help to drain the lymphatic system as well as improving the overall condition of their skin (provided a non-contaminated, organic vegetable oil is applied).

Massaging your baby's face can alleviate nasal congestion and help drain mucus from the nasal passages, which is extremely helpful for when your baby has a snuffle. Also, the Toe Rolling exercise (see Chapter 6) is excellent for helping to alleviate the symptoms of a cold and teething niggles, as this exercise is based around the traditional art of reflexology and the toes represent the face, including the nose, mouth, eyes and sinuses. Not only does massaging your baby's toes alleviate these symptoms, but it also has an immediate effect on their nervous system and encourages general well-being.

Relieves colic

Massaging your baby's tummy is a fantastic way to help regulate and strengthen the digestive system and alleviate wind, constipation and colic. It is very important to follow the guide in this book (see page 50) and massage their tummy in a clockwise direction as this is the direction in which the contents of the bowel move. By doing this you can help to move wind and faeces in the right direction. Furthermore, as massage can be relaxing, a stressed baby may find they are less anxious.

However, it is extremely important that you do not massage your baby while they are crying with pain. Crying is a 'negative cue' and a parent would not be listening to their baby if they ignored this and started to massage their tummy, regardless.

Improves sleep

Many babies find massage very soothing, and may even fall asleep immediately afterwards. You may find that your baby will sleep deeper and longer after a massage. If massage is introduced after their bath and as part of your baby's going-to-bed routine, it can help to release the tension in your baby, not to mention you!

The massage improves a baby's circulation, deepens and regulates the breathing, and increases the levels of oxygen in the bloodstream, which can lead to deeper sleep. Massage can help to make sleep-time more peaceful with a familiar pattern to it, which is very beneficial for fussy babies.

Natural pain relief

Generally, massage stimulates the production of oxytocin (a hormone secreted by both sexes), which is a natural pain reliever and induces a calming effect for your baby.

Helping your baby's cognitive development

Cognitive development is the process by which the brain develops the abilities to learn thinking, reasoning, memory and language skills during their early years and helps a child create an impression of the world around them.

These abilities start to develop in early infancy as the brain begins forming connections: during the first two years of life a baby's brain is developing at an exceptional rate. The pathways from the primitive brain to the frontal brain need to connect in the early years to enable a child to grow into a rational, reasoning and caring human being.

To help make these connections, a baby requires lots of positive and varied experiences such as new sights, sounds, smells and tactile stimulation. Massage is an excellent way of bringing new and positive experiences into a young baby's life as they offer the opportunity for positive touch and early play, especially when accompanied with lots of talking, music and singing of nursery rhymes.

2

the best time to massage

It is important to know the best time of the day for a massage and when it is not a good time. You also need to be aware of what your baby is telling you so you know when your baby is saying 'yes' or 'no' to massage.

To ensure that you have found the ideal time to massage your baby it is important to understand that your baby should only ever be massaged if they are happy and it is going to be a positive experience for them. This guarantees the emotional and physical benefits. If your baby is not happy or in the mood to be massaged then it can have a negative impact and the benefits will be lost.

You also need to be aware of the guidelines about the physical and medical conditions that may make massage for your baby inappropriate or harmful at that particular time.

How old should a baby be before massage can be introduced?

Generally, a good time to introduce the massage routine is after a baby has had their six-week health check. Although a six-week-old baby may still be quite sensitive to over-stimulation, they are at least becoming familiar with their surroundings at this stage and are more likely to be able to enjoy massage.

This doesn't mean that you can't introduce massage to your baby at all during the first few weeks. As massage can greatly help alleviate colic, you may wish to try the colic routine with your baby (see page 56).

What time of day is the best time to do baby massage?

Because babies naturally go through six different states of consciousness many times during the day, there will be occasions in the day when your baby will be more receptive to having a massage. By understanding these states, it becomes easier to anticipate when your baby might be ready to have a massage.

The six different states of consciousness are as follows:
* A deep sleep state
* A light sleep state
* A drowsy state
* An alert, awake state
* An alert, but fussy state
* Crying

An **alert, awake state** is a good time to see if a baby is happy to have a massage.

Understanding what your baby is telling you

Your baby will tell you how they are feeling and what they want by using 'non-verbal cues'. There is no 'recipe' of cues – all babies are individual and will have different ways of telling their parents what they want. Sometimes the cues will be very positive and your baby will let you know how happy they are. Other times, your baby will not be happy and will use negative cues to show you how they feel.

Is your baby saying 'yes' to massage?

When you are deciding whether your baby is saying 'yes' to massage, it is important to think about their non-verbal cues (e.g. look, alert, awake, bright and response) so that you can decide if it is a good time for them or not. Positive cues are more likely to indicate that your baby is saying 'yes' to massage; and the negative cues (fussy and crying) are probably a sign that it is not the right time for your baby, and they are saying 'no' to the activity.

Sometimes you might find it difficult to know whether your baby is saying 'yes' or 'no', particularly when their non-verbal cues are quite subtle and if you have not given it any thought before. Do not worry, this understanding will come in time, and you will find that if you have not understood what your baby is saying immediately, they will give out even stronger cues, making it quite clear how they are feeling.

During the massage routine it is vital that your baby is happy, in order for them to learn that these activities are fun and that when they say 'no' to massage, they are heard, listened to, and their feelings are respected. If a baby's 'no' cues are ignored, they will believe they do not have a voice and that their feelings are not worthy of attention. Also, babies that are not listened to often become withdrawn and generally less responsive.

You will probably find that when your baby is in an alert, awake state during the day, they are more likely to say 'yes' to massage, because they are keen to play and have fun with you during these periods. Many babies enjoy a massage just before or after a bath – you might find this also fits in with your routine. However, your baby may become quite excited after massage, so it may be that first thing in the morning is better for you both.

What is important is that it is right for your baby and you, so that massage is a thoroughly enjoyable experience.

When is it not a good time to do massage with your baby?

It is important to avoid doing massage with your baby if they:

* are asleep, tired, hungry, crying or fretful, because these are all '*no*' cues.
* are unwell, or have a raised temperature. Their immune system will need to be left to deal with the problem and not be over stimulated by massage.
* have an infectious skin condition, because this may aggravate the infected area. The most common skin infections in children are impetigo and ringworm. It is best to refrain from massage and skin-to-skin contact as there is a risk of cross-infection.
* are suffering from bruising, sprains or a fracture. It is advisable to refrain from massage until the injuries have healed completely and the swelling has gone down. It may be possible for the unaffected areas to be massaged.
* have open, weeping wounds and rashes or have an unhealed navel. Breaks in the skin may become infected if massaged and this might cause discomfort and pain.
* are suffering from jaundice, as their liver is most likely not functioning as it should. Refrain from massage until the liver is functioning correctly.
* have received vaccinations within the previous three days. Vaccinations have an impact on the immune system, as vaccines trigger the immune system to produce antibodies in a similar manner to that of the actual disease. Because massage is stimulating and has an impact on the immune system, it is necessary to have a break from these activities, so that your baby's body is not overloaded or over-stimulated while it is trying to deal with the vaccinations given.

* have been diagnosed with brittle bone disease. The bones in children suffering from this disease can be so brittle that they break with normal handling.

Generally, after surgery, refrain from massaging the affected area for at least eight weeks to allow the wound to heal. However other areas of your baby's body could be massaged once they have recovered from having an operation. Only massage the unaffected areas once your baby has been given the all clear by the surgeon or GP.

3

preparing for massage

Before any massage begins it is important to make sure the environment is just right to create a peaceful atmosphere. If you have ever received a therapeutic treatment yourself, you will be aware of how important the ambience of the therapy room is, the service provided by the therapist and the standard of the equipment used and how it enhanced your experience, or not as the case may be! This is exactly the same for your baby – with the right atmosphere you can enjoy a safe, undisturbed and special time together.

It is easy to create the perfect massage space for you and your baby when you know the equipment you need, how to set up the room and how to prepare yourself for a relaxed and fun massage session.

Preparing the environment for massage

There is nothing very complicated about preparing for baby massage and it doesn't cost the earth. Before any massage begins it is important to make sure that the environment is just right to create a peaceful atmosphere so that the experience is as relaxing as possible. The space will need to be comfortable, quiet and somewhere that will have few distractions.

Preparing for massage

The room

* **Warmth:** Choose a room that will be warm enough for your baby to be naked.
* **Light:** Use natural daylight, where possible. If not, introduce soft, subtle lighting.
* **Noise:** Try to ensure the room is as quiet as possible.
* **Music:** Introducing soothing music can really help to create a relaxing atmosphere for both you and your baby.
* **Smells:** Part of the bonding process is a baby becoming familiar with its parent's natural smell and vice versa. Try to eliminate any artificial smells such as perfumes, air fresheners or aromatherapy oils.

Equipment

Before the massage begins, prepare the following items:
* changing mat or large thick towel for your baby
* CD player and relaxing music
* a pillow for you to sit on
* tissues, baby wipes or a spare towel for little accidents
* small bottle of massage oil at room temperature
* teddy or toy and a small mirror to amuse older babies
* fresh nappy for when the massage is complete
* a drink for your baby to have when the massage is over
* this book!

Getting yourself ready for massage

Not only do you need to prepare the room, the equipment and your baby, but *you* need to be prepared too. It is vital to be as relaxed as possible before giving your baby a massage. Sometimes, this is easier said than done!

* **Be comfortable:** It is advisable to wear comfortable clothing, as you will be spending lots of time sitting on the floor when massaging. Wearing a T-shirt or loose top may allow for easier movement and ensures that you do not become too warm.
* **Jewellery:** Remove any jewellery that may scratch your baby's skin or dangle in their face.
* **Hands and nails:** Ensure that your hands are washed before the massage and any nail snags have been filed away. Take care to use only the pads of your fingers when massaging your baby as long nails, in particular, may cause discomfort.
* **Hair:** If you have long hair it is advisable to have it tied back during the massage; this will ensure it does not dangle on your baby's skin and tickle.
* **Position:** You need to be aware of your sitting position so that you are comfortable when doing the massage routine. Use a cushion or beanbag and, if possible, rest against a wall, or a sturdy piece of furniture.
* **Relaxation:** Consider using a relaxation technique before massaging your baby.

4

choosing oils for baby massage

For massage to be a comfortable experience for your baby it is vital to use a massage medium, such as oil. This ensures that there is no friction and that your hands do not drag your baby's skin when carrying out the massage strokes.

However, there is a vast range of oils that are marketed for massage use and many of these are, unfortunately, unsuitable for babies. It is important that you understand which oils are safe for baby massage, and that you learn about those that are best avoided or potentially harmful.

In addition to knowing the best massage oil for baby massage, you will also need to be aware of where to buy them, how to store them for safe use and how to recognize when to discard them for a new, fresh supply.

The best oils to use for massage

For massage to be enjoyable and comfortable for your baby it is best to use a massage medium, such as oil. The oil allows the massage movements and strokes to be carried out without causing friction to your baby's skin; without oil the massage can be irritating, especially for a sensitive newborn. It is recommended, where possible, that an organic or cold-pressed vegetable oil is used because they are as natural as possible and contain little or no preservatives or additives. This is especially important as babies may ingest some of the oil during the massage. Natural vegetable oils:

* allow the skin to breathe
* nourish and moisturize the skin
* are easily absorbed into the skin
* are unscented
* are natural and safe.

Vegetable oils

* **Organic oil** that is truly organic will have been grown in strict organic conditions, starting with the seed, nuts or fruits and the condition of soil. There must be no use of pesticides and an oil extraction process that is free of chemicals. These oils may be difficult to find and can be expensive.
* **Cold-pressed oil** is produced by using high pressure to squeeze out the oil from soft, oily seeds such as sunflower. For harder seeds, more pressure is used to crush the seed, which generates some heat (and may alter the oil). After crushing, the shells are removed by filters and the oil is natural. (Some oils may be further refined after cold-pressing.)
* **Refined oils** are made from the vegetable pulp that remains after cold-pressing. This vegetable pulp still contains some oil and is refined either by high temperatures, high pressures or may be treated with steam or solvents. This process alters the oil somewhat to remove allergens and impurities, which can help to make it hypoallergenic and safer to use with babies that are prone to allergic reactions or who have weaker immune systems.

What to choose?

Parents will have a number of reasons for choosing a particular oil, but careful consideration should be given to:

* availability
* the skin type of your baby
* risk of allergic reactions
* how the oil will be stored.

Sunflower oil (*Helianthus annuus*)

Sunflower oil is excellent for baby massage; it has a light texture and does not leave the skin feeling greasy.

Grape seed oil (*Vitis vinifera*)

This oil is made from the hard stone of the grape and is highly refined due to the manufacture process and has little odour, is good for slippage and isn't too greasy when applied to the skin.

Fractionated Coconut oil (*Cocos nucifera*)

This is a refined oil that has been produced from the original solid fat coconut oil being heat treated. The fractionization of the oil removes all potential allergens, mould spores and impurities leaving pure, perfume-free oil that remains as a liquid. This oil will not go off as quickly as other oils and is excellent for slippage in baby massage.

Cooking oils

Cooking oils such as sunflower and grape seed purchased from a supermarket are highly-refined oils (food grade). They have been purified to enable them to have consistent colour and a longer shelf life.

Oils to avoid

Nut oils

Nut oils, such as almond and peanut, are generally not recommended for baby massage. The Anaphylaxis Campaign suggests that peanut is a high allergy risk in the UK.

Mineral oils

There are a number of mineral oils and commercially available 'baby massage oils or gels' on the market but it is recommended that these are not used for baby massage. Commercially available mineral oil/gel is a highly processed by-product of petroleum (paraffin wax). Baby mineral oil contains chemicals and preservatives and is not broken down by the body's digestive system. It has already been mentioned that it may be ingested by the baby during massage as it may be on their hands.

We strongly recommend that you avoid using mineral oil at all costs. Regular use causes the skin to dry out.

Artificially scented oil

Some commercial baby massage vegetable oils and gels often contain artificial perfumes. It is important to avoid these particular oils because they may contain chemicals that may be harmful when ingested. As the artificial scents are often quite a strong smell, your baby may find them overpowering and over-stimulating for the senses. Furthermore, the scent prevents the baby from smelling their parent's natural scent.

Essential oils

Owing to the popularity of aromatherapy, many products containing various essential oils are appearing on the market. The oils that are considered to be a softer option, such as lavender and tea tree, are not safe to use on prepubescent children as it has been proven that the hormonal activities in the oil may trigger abnormal breast development in young children. The chemical content of essential oils is absorbed into the body via the olfactory system (nose and lungs) and 60 per cent of substances massaged in to the skin are absorbed into the blood stream.

To date there is *NO* research to validate that the use of essential oils with infants is indeed safe.

Where to buy oil

* Where possible, buy massage oil from a reputable supplier.
* If buying a vegetable oil from a supermarket, look for organic, cold-pressed varieties.

Storage of oils

* It is best to buy organic and cold-pressed vegetable oils in small quantities, as the shelf life is limited (a 50 ml bottle should last several massage sessions).
* Store oils in a cool, dark place such as a larder.
* Leave the oil to warm to room temperature before massage.
* Discard oil that has gone rancid (oil that has gone off has a rather unpleasant odour).
* Do not use old oil that has been left for a while as the air in the bottle will oxidize the oil and it may become rancid.
* Discard any oil that has been decanted from a large bottle into a sterilized dish for a massage session. Do not return unused oil back into the original bottle as this could potentially contaminate the oil with bacteria.

5

the massage routine – getting started

Getting started

* Choose a time when your baby is happy to be massaged.
* Prepare the room: remember
  * subdued lighting
  * warm room
  * no overpowering fragrances
  * quiet space.
* Collect equipment, e.g. oil, wipes, towels, etc.
* Have this book to hand to learn the routine.
* Use a CD player and choose relaxing music.
* Remove sharp jewellery and wash hands.
* Be mindful of your own comfort.

The massage routine

The following chapters (Chapters 6–10) give parents a step-by-step massage routine to follow with their baby once they are ready to experience the full massage.

Each chapter covers the strokes for one body area and allows you to learn and practise these strokes during the following week. If time permits, try to practise the massage strokes on a daily basis at a time that is suitable for both you and your baby. This will help you feel comfortable with the strokes and help your baby to become accustomed to the new strokes too. Each stroke has been given a suitable name to help you remember the full routine.

Try to follow the chapters for the massage routine in the order given. Starting with the legs allows your baby to become accustomed to the massage strokes, on what could be considered the least sensitive part of their body. The rest of the routine naturally follows up the front of the body and then on to the back.

Each week, start with the strokes for the new body area and then consolidate the body area(s) that have been learned the previous week(s). This allows you to learn the new strokes first before moving on to and practising the previously learned ones, should your baby be too tired to carry on. If you always started the massage with the legs, while working through the learning programme, then you might find it very difficult to progress to the new strokes if your baby becomes tired.

The learning programme

Week 1 – Legs

Week 2 – Stomach and Legs

Week 3 – Chest, Legs and Stomach

Week 4 – Back, Legs, Stomach and Chest

Week 5 – Head and Face, Legs, Stomach, Chest and Back

Week 6 – The Full Routine: Legs, Stomach, Chest, Head and Face, Back

Each chapter will contain:

* step-by-step instructions accompanied with line drawings to guide you through the routine

* hints and tips on safety during massage
* suggested nursery rhymes that enhance the enjoyment of each stroke
* alternative positions
* benefits for the baby.

The reasons behind the sequencing of strokes

Legs

To the untrained eye the leg sequence will appear to jump from one leg to the other and back again without good reason. However, there is indeed a very good reason for this. A baby's concentration span is very limited and although they may say 'Yes' to massage to begin with, within a few minutes of starting the massage this may change. If only one leg has received massage then the baby may feel slightly imbalanced as the massaged leg will feel relaxed while the other will still be carrying some tension. The sequence in Chapter 6 prevents this happening should the massage be cut short for whatever reason.

Back/head and face

Young babies often assume that 'food' is on offer when their face is touched due to the rooting reflex. As they develop and settle into a feeding pattern this becomes less frequent, so by leaving the head and face sequence until Week 5, this allows for the younger baby to progress to this stage.

Applying the oil

Patch-testing the oil

As a precaution, it is always preferable to do a patch-test first to check that the baby does not have an allergic reaction to the oil you have chosen.

* Rub a small amount of oil on the inside of your baby's wrist.
* Leave for 15 minutes.
* If there is no reaction, use this oil for the massage.

* If skin becomes inflamed and irritated, wash the area thoroughly with warm water and pat dry.
* DO NOT use an oil that causes a reaction.

Using oil during massage
* Warm the oil to room temperature for a short time before the massage session.
* There needs to be enough oil to lubricate the whole area to be massaged (usually about the size of a ten pence piece).
* Put the oil in the palm of one hand.
* Rub your hands together to warm the oil.
* On the first application it may be necessary to apply a little more as some of the oil may be absorbed by your hands if you have particularly dry skin.
* Apply the warmed oil gently to the area to be massaged.

Gauging the correct pressure

There is no right or wrong pressure when massaging; every baby is different. Some babies quite like a vigorous massage while others would find this far too stimulating and would probably start to cry and show negative cues. However, even for babies that do not like a very firm touch, it is important that your touch is firm enough not to tickle them. Tickling can be far too stimulating and unpleasant for a young baby.

While massaging your baby it is important, where you can, to keep at least one hand in constant contact with your baby's body. This makes sure that you do not startle them when you place your hand or hands on a part of their body that they are not expecting to be touched. Keeping one hand in contact with them will reassure them and make the massage far more relaxing.

After massage

After the massage has finished, it is advisable for parents to pay particular notice to the following:
* Offer your baby a drink as they may be thirsty.

* Wash or wipe your hands to remove all residual oil before attempting to move your baby.
* Wipe residual oil from your baby's skin, especially if bathing afterwards.
* Wrap or dress your baby after the massage to ensure they do not become cold.
* Often babies become sleepy after the massage; allow them to sleep or relax.
* Never allow a baby with oiled skin to be exposed to sunlight after a massage, as the oil may cause the skin to burn.

Asking permission

It is important to ask your baby if they would like a massage before you begin any massage. This will ensure that your baby feels heard and their feelings are respected.

Before undressing your baby for massage, ask permission by:
* placing both hands gently on your baby's chest and rubbing gently in a circular motion
* looking into your baby's eyes
* asking your baby in a playful, melodious tone, 'Would you like a massage today (name)?'

In the first week of practice your baby may not respond very clearly or even at all to this question as this is new to them too and obviously they do not understand what they are being asked. Because of this you may feel unsure whether to carry on with the massage or not at first, but very soon your baby will let you know, in no uncertain terms, whether they are happy with the massage or not.

With regular massage your baby will come to recognize that this question is the signal for massage and then respond accordingly. If they want a massage they usually become very excited and display many of the positive cues mentioned in Chapter 2.

The opening and closing sequence

Once your baby has given their consent for massage, the next step is to perform the wonderful opening stroke of the Velvet Cloak (see opposite). This stroke is done when your baby is still clothed and signals to them that the massage is soon to begin. It also prepares their whole body for the massage. Once you have done this you can then undress your baby ready for the massage.

At the end of the massage session, no matter how much you manage to do, it is always good practice to finish with a Velvet Cloak too. This stroke is perfect for signalling the start and end of a massage session.

Asking permission

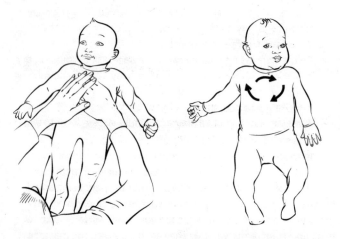

Figure 5.1 *Asking permission.*   **Figure 5.2** *Direction for asking permission.*

1 Ask permission before undressing your baby.
2 Place your hands lightly on your baby's chest, rub gently in a circular motion and ask permission from your baby to massage them.

The Velvet Cloak (to begin and end all massage sessions)

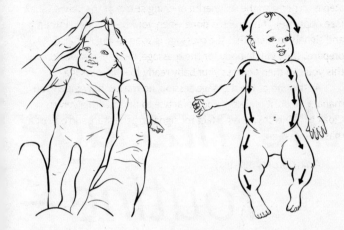

Figure 5.3 *The Velvet Cloak.*   **Figure 5.4** *Direction for the Velvet Cloak.*

1 Bring both hands to the top of your baby's head.
2 Using the flat of your whole hand, lightly stroke down the sides of the body to the feet.
3 Repeat three times.

6

the massage routine – the legs and feet

These are the strokes that we advise you use to practise with your baby for the first week of your massage time together. We consider the legs to be the least sensitive part of the body so if you haven't carried out massage before, your baby is more likely to have a positive, first massage experience.

Once you've asked for the permission of your baby and they have indicated that they are happy to have a massage then begin with the Velvet Cloak stroke (see page 31) before starting the legs and feet routine.

As all the strokes have names to help you learn the routine, listed below are the strokes you will carry out in this part of the routine.

* Upward Leg Glide
* Gentle Leg Knead
* Sole Stroke
* Toe Rolling
* Jelly Roll
* Double Leg Lift

Enjoy!

Upward Leg Glide

Position

* Baby is lying on their back for all leg and foot strokes.

Tips

* Remember to ask permission in the first week of the learning programme.
* Remember to do the Velvet Cloak in the first week of the learning programme.
* Remove your baby's clothes.
* Apply oil to both legs and feet (about the size of a ten pence piece in the palm).
* Take care to glide very gently on the downward stroke. This prevents any undue pressure on the delicate valves in the baby's veins.

Suggested nursery rhyme

Jack and Jill
Went up the hill
To fetch a pail of water
Jack fell down
And broke his crown
And Jill came tumbling after!

Benefits

* Promotes body awareness.
* Soothes sensory nerve endings, helping your baby to relax.

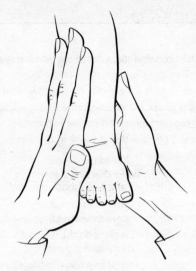

Figure 6.1 *Upward Leg Glide hand position.*

Figure 6.2 *Direction for Upward Leg Glide.*

1 Slightly raise your baby's leg by supporting one ankle with your hand.
2 Using the palm of your hand, stroke up the leg from the ankle to the top of the thigh firmly and glide down the back of the leg from the buttocks to the ankle, gently.
3 Swap hands and stroke up the leg again.
4 Repeat three times with both hands.

Gentle Leg Knead

Tips

* Stay with the same leg, as with the Upward Leg Glide.
* Take care to glide very gently over the knee.
* Take care to glide very gently on the downward stroke.

Suggested nursery rhyme

Knead the dough
Knead the dough
When that side's done
It's over we go!
Knead the dough
Knead the dough
Bake it well
And watch it grow.

Adapted from *Knead the Dough* by Lowell Herbert

Benefits

* Increases oxygen and nutrients to the cells.
* Encourages efficient circulation and lymph drainage.

Figure 6.3 *Gentle Leg Kneed hand position.*

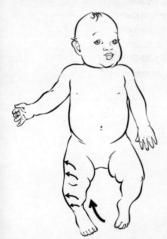

Figure 6.4 *Direction of the Gentle Leg Kneed.*

1 Slightly raise your baby's leg by supporting their ankle.
2 Starting at the ankle – using the whole of your hand (thumb on top of the leg, fingers at the back) – knead one side of the leg towards the knee.
3 **Gently glide the thumb over the knee.**
4 Continue to knead from just above the knee to the hip.
5 Gently glide your hand down the back of the leg to the ankle to maintain contact.
6 Swap hands and knead the other side of the leg.
7 Repeat three times.

Repeat the Upward Leg Glide and the Gentle Leg Knead on the other leg before moving on to the feet.

Sole Stroke

Tips

* Stay with this leg.
* Take care not to tickle.
* For babies that have had invasive medical interventions, such as an intravenous cannula, take care if the area on the foot is still sore and be mindful that your baby maybe 'touch defensive' in this area.
* Take care not to twist the toes when rolling them.

Suggested nursery rhyme

Windscreen wipers
What do you do all day?
Swish, swosh
Swish, swosh
I wipe the rain away
Windscreen wipers
What do you do all day?
Swish, swosh
Swish, swosh
I wipe the rain away.

Benefits

* Increases circulation to the feet.
* Opens up the energy channels in reflexology zones.

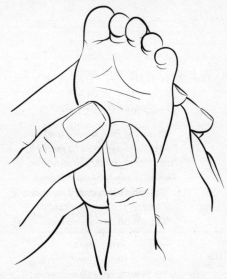

Figure 6.5 *Sole Stroke hand position.*

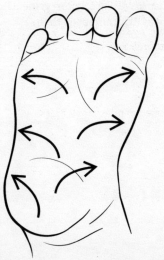

1. With the leg slightly raised cup your baby's foot with both hands.
2. Alternating your thumbs, stroke the sole of the foot, from heel to toes, fanning the thumbs from the centre to the side.
3. Repeat three times.

Figure 6.6 *Direction for the Sole Stroke.*

Toe Rolling

Tips

* Do not twist the toe when rolling.
* Take care to pull the toe very gently.

Suggested nursery rhyme

(Starting with the big toe)
This little piggy went to market
This little piggy stayed at home
This little piggy had a massage
And this little piggy didn't want one
And this little piggy said
'Oh, oh, oh I want one too!'

Benefits

* An opportunity for baby to visually observe their own feet, fostering body awareness.
* An ideal time to introduce language and counting games.
* Works on the reflexology areas that correspond to the head, sinuses and teeth.

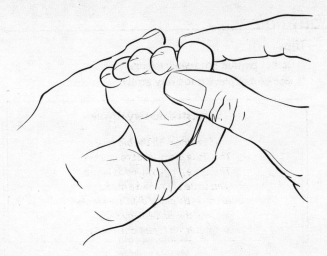

Figure 6.7 *Toe Rolling hand position.*

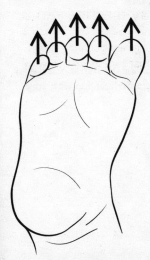

1 Still keeping the leg slightly raised, cup your baby's foot with one hand.
2 With the other hand gently roll each toe between finger and thumb from the base of the toe to the tip, starting with the big toe.
3 Gently hold each toe at the end of the roll.
Now repeat Sole Stroke and Toe Rolling on the other foot.

Figure 6.8 *Direction for Toe Rolling.*

After the foot strokes are complete on both feet, repeat Upward Leg Glide on both legs before moving on to Jelly Roll.

Tips

* It is important not to roll your baby's knee.
* Babies really love this stroke, so sing with gusto!

Suggested nursery rhyme

Jelly on a plate
Jelly on a plate
Wibble, wobble,
Wibble wobble
Jelly on a plate
Jelly on a plate
Jelly on a plate
Wibble, wobble,
Wibble wobble
Jelly on a plate.

Benefits

* Improves suppleness and elasticity.
* Induces relaxation by literally 'rolling out' tension in the leg.
* This is a great opportunity for you to have fun with your baby.

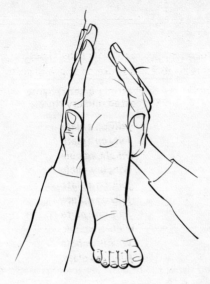

Figure 6.9 *Jelly Roll hand position.*

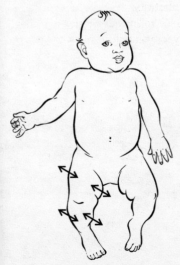

Figure 6.10 *Direction for the Jelly Roll.*

1 Support one of your baby's legs upright by holding the thigh between both hands (as though making a dough sausage).

2 Roll the thigh between both of your hands.

3 Continue rolling up to the knee.

4 Gently slide your hands over the knee to the calf.

5 Continue rolling up to the ankle.

6 Repeat three times.
   Change leg and repeat.

Double Leg Lift

Tip

* Take care to stroke gently down the back of the legs.

Suggested nursery rhyme

Baa baa black sheep
Have you any wool?
Yes Sir, Yes Sir
Three bags full
One for the master
One for the dame
And one for the little boy
Who lives down the lane.

Benefits

* A good stroke to finish the leg and foot massage.
* Gently stretches muscles.
* Induces relaxation.

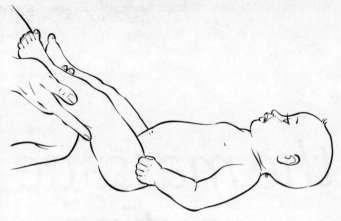

Figure 6.11 *Double Leg Lift hand position.*

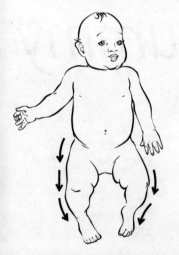

1 Supporting the buttocks with both hands, gently stroke down the back of the legs to the ankles, giving a little lift and pull at the end.
2 Gently lower your baby's legs to the ground.

Figure 6.12 *Direction for the Double Leg Lift.*

7

the massage routine – the tummy

These are the strokes that we advise you to practise with your baby for the second week of your massage time together. To ensure that the massage is enjoyable and safe, it is vital that you massage your baby's stomach in a clockwise direction to work with the digestive system.

Once you've asked for the permission of your baby and they have indicated they are happy to have a massage then begin with the Velvet Cloak stroke (see page 31) before starting the tummy routine.

Listed below are the strokes you will carry out in this part of the routine:

* Tummy Hug
* Tummy Circle
* Daisy Wheel
* Windmill
* Knee Hug

If your baby is happy to continue, remember to include the leg strokes you learned in the previous chapter at the end. But the new strokes should always come first.

As your baby's nappy is off, remember to keep a spare towel handy as the tummy strokes can often result in a purge!

Tummy Hug

Position

* Baby is lying on their back for all of the tummy routine.

Tips

* Remember to ask permission when in Week 2 of the learning programme.
* Remember to do the Velvet Cloak when in Week 2 of the programme.
* Remove your baby's clothes.
* Apply oil to the tummy area.
* Remove the nappy for ease with strokes.
* **It is very important to remember – always stroke the tummy area in a clockwise direction.**
* **Do not press on the rib cage when performing the tummy strokes.**

Suggested nursery rhyme

Pizza, pizza – it's a treat.
Pizza, pizza – fun to eat!
Stringy, gooey cheese so yummy;
Pepperoni in my tummy.
Pizza, pizza – it's a treat.
Pizza, pizza – fun to eat!

Benefits

* This is the 'opening' movement and indicates to your baby that the tummy massage is about to begin.

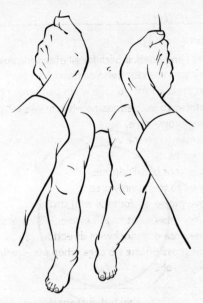

Figure 7.1 *The Tummy Hug hand position.*

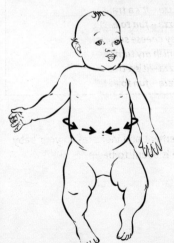

1 Hold your baby by moulding your hands around their lower back and sides, your fingers not quite touching under your baby's body.
2 Return both your hands from the back to the middle of the tummy area.
3 Stroke just below the rib cage.
4 Repeat three times.

Figure 7.2 *Direction for the Tummy Hug.*

Tummy Circle

Tips

* It is very important to remember – always stroke the tummy area in a *clockwise* direction.
* Do not press on the rib cage when performing the tummy strokes.

Suggested nursery rhyme

Round and round the garden
Like a teddy bear.
I'd better put my wellies on
Coz it's muddy out there!

Benefits

* A relaxing stroke that helps to warm the tissue in the tummy area.
* Gently increases the circulation to the tummy.

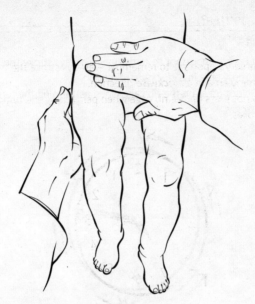

Figure 7.3 *The Tummy Circle hand position.*

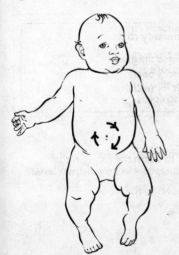

1 Using the pads of your index and middle fingers, stroke a wide circle around the tummy button in a clockwise direction.
2 Repeat three times.

Figure 7.4 *Direction for the Tummy Circle.*

Daisy Wheel

Tips

* It is very important to remember – always stroke the tummy area in a ***clockwise*** direction.
* Do not press on the rib cage when performing the tummy strokes.

Suggested nursery rhyme

Ring a ring o'roses
A pocketful of posies
ah-tishoo, ah-tishoo
We all fall down.

Benefits

* This is a slightly deeper stroke than the Tummy Circle and helps to move along trapped wind and helps alleviate constipation.

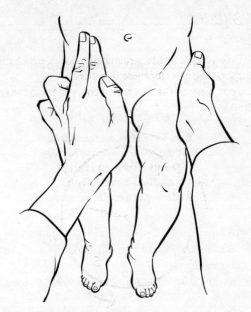

Figure 7.5 *The Daisy Wheel hand position.*

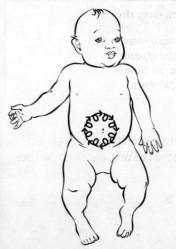

1 Using the pads of your index and middle fingers, make small circles, like the petals of a flower, around the tummy button in a clockwise direction.
2 Repeat three times.
3 Finish with three Tummy Circles.

Figure 7.6 *Direction for the Daisy Wheel.*

Windmill

Tip

* Take care not to press on the rib cage when performing the tummy strokes.

Suggested nursery rhyme

Blow wind blow, and go mill go,
That the Miller may grind his corn.
That the Baker may take it,
And into bread make it,
And bring us a loaf in the morn.

Benefits

* This is a soothing stroke that will induce relaxation of the tummy area.
* Helps with bowel movements and alleviates trapped wind.

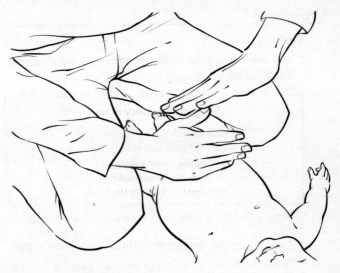

Figure 7.7 *The Windmill hand position.*

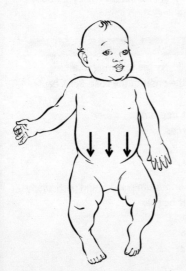

1 Imagine your hands are like two paddles.
2 Using the flat of both hands, stroke from beneath the rib cage to the top of the legs.
3 Stroke down with one hand at a time like the paddles of a windmill.
4 Repeat six times (three times for each hand).

Figure 7.8 *Direction for the Windmill.*

Knee Hug

Tips

* Take care not to press too hard on the legs and the hip area.
* Avoid pressing the knees in to the tummy area, but allow the hip joints to open in their natural position (so the legs are slightly parted).

Suggested game

Peekaboo! I see you!

Benefits

* This is a traditional yoga movement which helps release trapped wind.
* Relaxes tummy muscles.
* Gently stretches the muscles of the lower back and buttocks.
* Good opportunity for playful interaction with your baby when performed with the Peekaboo game.

Colic routine

To help babies suffering from colic, try the following routine approximately one hour before the onset of the colic. See Chapter 1 for more information.

* Tummy Circle – Repeat three times.
* Windmill – Repeat six times.
* Knee Hug – Once.

Repeat this sequence three times.

Repeat the whole routine three or our times a day and particularly an hour before the time the colic begins.

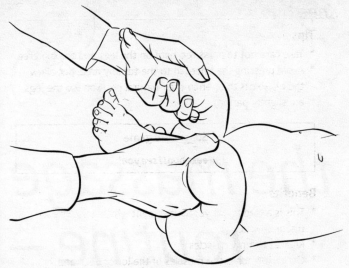

Figure 7.9 *The Knee Hug hand position.*

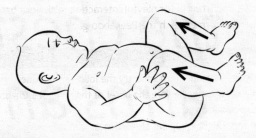

Figure 7.10 *Direction for the Knee Hug.*

1 Support your baby's ankles and lower legs in each of your hands.
2 Bend their legs at the knee and very gently bring the thighs up towards the tummy.
3 Hold for a count of six.
4 Relax the legs down again.
5 Repeat three times.

8

the massage routine – the chest, arms and hands

These are the strokes that we advise you to practise with your baby for the third week of your massage time together. To ensure that the massage is enjoyable and safe, the massage strokes for the chest area should not encroach on the tummy area.

Once you've asked for the permission of your baby and they have indicated they are happy to have a massage then begin with the Velvet Cloak stroke (see page 31) before starting the chest routine.

These are the strokes you will carry out in this part of the routine:

* Chest and Arm Glide
* Loving Heart
* Loving Kisses
* Finger Rolling
* Chest and Arm Glide (again)

If your baby is happy to continue, remember to include the leg and tummy strokes that you have already learned. As before, the new strokes should always come first.

Don't worry if your baby is too busy sucking fingers for you to carry out the full massage; come back to these when they are less busy!

Chest and Arm Glide

Position

* Lay your baby on their back for all chest and arm strokes.

Tips

* Remember to ask permission when in Week 3 of the learning programme.
* Remember to do the Velvet Cloak when in Week 3 of the programme.
* Remove your baby's clothes.
* Apply oil to the chest area.
* You can leave your baby's nappy on just for the chest strokes.
* Some babies are not comfortable with their chest, arms or hands being massaged. Be guided by your baby's cues.
* Take care not to start below the ribs as this may cause some discomfort when gliding up the chest.

Suggested nursery rhyme

Baa baa black sheep
Have you any wool?
Yes Sir, Yes Sir
Three bags full
One for the master
One for the dame
And one for the little boy
Who lives down the lane.

Benefits

* Emphasizes body awareness and wholeness.

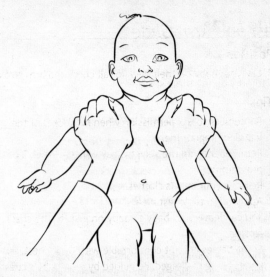

Figure 8.1 *The Chest and Arm Glide hand position.*

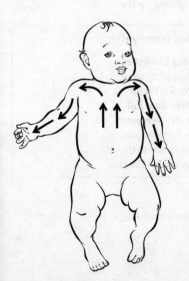

1 Place both your hands flat on your baby's chest.
2 Slide your hands up the chest.
3 Cup the shoulders.
4 Gently stroke down the arms to the wrists.
5 Finish by opening your baby's palms gently with your thumbs.
6 Repeat three times.

Figure 8.2 *Direction for the Chest and Arm Glide.*

Tips

* Refrain from bringing your hands down to your baby's tummy during these strokes.

Suggested nursery rhyme

Hickory Dickory Dock,
The mouse ran up the clock;
The clock struck one
And down he did run,
Hickory Dickory Dock.

Benefits

* This stroke helps relax and tone chest muscles.
* Improves circulation, lymph drainage and breathing capacity.

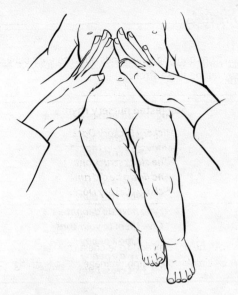

Figure 8.3 *The Loving Heart hand position.*

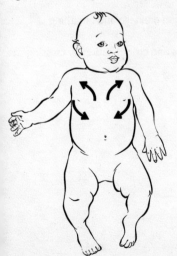

1 Lay both hands on your baby's chest.
2 Slide your hands up the middle of their chest towards the shoulders.
3 Cup the shoulders gently.
4 In a gentle sweeping movement, follow down the sides of the chest. This stroke resembles a heart-shape.
5 Repeat three times.

Figure 8.4 *Direction for the Loving Heart.*

Tip

* Take care to keep one hand in contact with your baby at all times.

Suggested nursery rhyme

Hot cross buns
Hot cross buns
One a penny
Two a penny
Hot cross buns
If you have no daughters
Give them to your sons
One a penny
Two a penny
Hot cross buns.

Benefits

* Improves circulation, lymph drainage and breathing capacity.
* Improves body awareness and co-ordination by crossing the midline of the body.

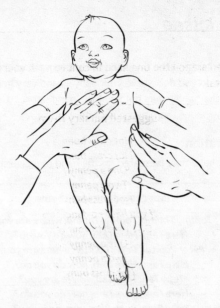

Figure 8.5 *Loving Kisses hand position.*

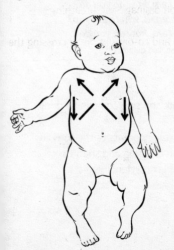

1 Place both your hands either side of your baby's rib cage, near their waist.
2 Using one hand at a time slide your hand up to the opposite shoulder.
3 Cup the shoulder.
4 Slide your hands down the side of the rib cage.
5 Using the other hand, repeat on the opposite side of the chest.
6 Repeat each hand three times.

Figure 8.6 *Direction for Loving Kisses.*

Finger Rolling

Tips

* When singing the rhyme to this movement, at the prompt 'how do you do?' shake your baby's hand very gently.
* Smaller babies may not want the hand strokes, keep trying to introduce them at regular intervals.

Adaptation

* Your baby may be seated for the hand massage strokes.

Suggested nursery rhyme

Tommy Thumb, Tommy Thumb, where are you?
Here I am, Here I am, how do you do?
Peter Pointer, Peter Pointer, where are you?
Here I am, Here I am, how do you do?
Toby Tall, Toby Tall, where are you?
Here I am, Here I am, how do you do?
Ruby Ring, Ruby Ring, where are you?
Here I am, Here I am, how do you do?
Baby Small, Baby Small, where are you?
Here I am, Here I am, how do you do?

(Last verse said quietly.)

Benefits

* Provides opportunity to talk and sing and can be done anywhere at anytime.
* The hands mirror the reflexology points of the toes so Finger Rolling can help with teething and snuffles.
* Good for opening up and relaxing clenched fists.

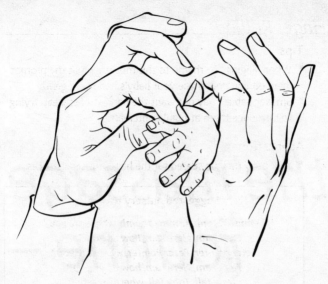

Figure 8.7 *Finger Rolling hand position.*

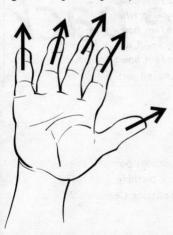

1 Support your baby's hand in one of your hands and perform the movement with your free hand.
2 Start with the thumb.
3 Roll each of your baby's fingers between your forefinger and thumb from the base of their finger to the tip.
4 At the tip give a gentle hold and move onto the next finger.

Figure 8.8 *Direction for Finger Rolling.*

Finish the chest routine with another Chest and Arm Glide (see pages 60–61).

the massage
routine –
the back

These are the strokes that we advise you to practise with your baby for the fourth week of your massage time together. To ensure that the massage is enjoyable and safe, the massage strokes for the back should not include the spine, as this is a delicate area of the body.

Once you've asked for the permission of your baby and they have indicated they are happy to have a massage, begin with the Velvet Cloak stroke (see page 31) before starting this routine.

These are the strokes you will cover in the routine for the back:

* Back Velvet Cloak
* Complete Back Soother
* Glide and Circle
* Glide and Stretch
* Cat's Paws
* Back Velvet Cloak

If your baby is happy to continue, remember to include the leg, tummy, chest and arm strokes. As before, the new strokes should always come first.

If your baby is unhappy about lying on their tummy, you can try these strokes holding your baby over your shoulder and massaging one side of the back at a time. (Remember to support your own back.)

Back Velvet Cloak

Position

* Lay your baby on their front, in the Prone Position, with head to one side for all the back strokes.

Tips

* Remember to ask permission when in Week 4 of the learning programme.
* Remember to do the Velvet Cloak when in Week 4 of the programme.
* Remove your baby's clothes.
* This is a good stroke to oil the back completely before the back massage begins.
* **It is extremely important to work on either side of the spine, not on the spine itself, when massaging the back.**
* Use the alternative position with baby on your lap if they want to be close.
* If your baby is on your lap, place a small mirror on the floor beneath them for added fun.

Suggested nursery rhyme

Substitute baby's name in [name]

**Rain, rain, go away,
Come again another day;
Little [name] wants to play.
Rain, rain, go away,
Come again another day.
Rain, rain, go to Spain.
Never show your face again.**

Benefits

* This is the 'opening' stroke for the back massage and helps your baby to become familiar with touch to their back.

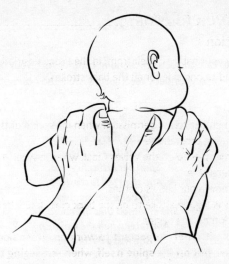

Figure 9.1 *The Back Velvet Cloak hand position.*

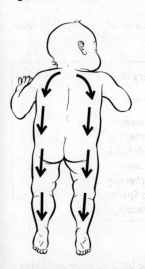

Figure 9.2 *Direction for the Back Velvet Cloak.*

1 Stroke from your baby's shoulders down to the ankles.
2 Remember to lighten the stroke from the buttocks to the ankles.
3 Repeat three times.

Complete Back Soother

Tip

* Take care to keep one hand in contact with your baby at all times, so your baby feels secure while they cannot see you.

Suggested nursery rhyme

The little fuzzy caterpillar,
Curled up on a leaf,
Spun her little chrysalis,
And then fell fast asleep.
While she was sleeping,
She dreamed that she could fly,
And later when she woke up
She was a butterfly!

Benefits

* Soothing and relaxing.
* This stroke provides full body integration and feelings of wholeness and connection for the baby.

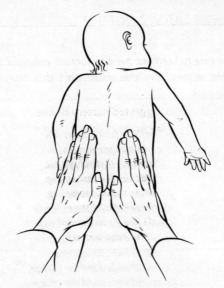

Figure 9.3 *The Complete Back Soother hand position.*

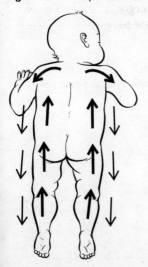

1 Start at your baby's ankles, stroke up both legs and continue up their back (fingers either side of the spine).
2 Lightly cup their shoulders and stroke down the arms.
3 Slide hands back to the shoulders.
4 Slide hands down to the ankles along the sides of the back and the legs (lighten the stroke from the buttocks to the ankles).
5 Repeat three times.

Figure 9.4 *Direction for the Complete Back Soother.*

Tip

* Take care not to hold the sides of your baby during this stroke, as this may tickle when your hands move up their back.

Suggested nursery rhyme

Go in and out the window,
Go in and out the window,
Go in and out the window,
As we have done before.
Go up and down the staircase,
Go up and down the staircase,
Go up and down the staircase,
As we have done before.
Go round and round the village,
Go round and round the village,
Go round and round the village,
As we have done before.

Benefits

* Increases circulation to the muscles along the spine.
* Assists the development of muscle tone and postural support.
* Induces feelings of relaxation.

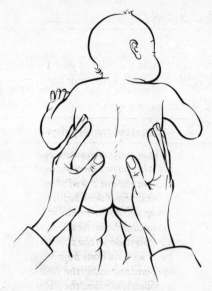

Figure 9.5 *Glide and Circle hand position.*

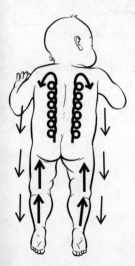

1 Place both your hands flat on your baby's ankles and glide your hands up their legs over the buttocks.
2 With the pads of the thumbs or the first two fingers, make tiny circles either side of the spine up to the shoulders.
3 Before working on the back, you may wish to circle the thumbs on the buttocks; this is optional.
4 Glide hands back to the ankles (remember to lighten the stroke from the buttocks to the ankles).
5 Repeat three times.

Figure 9.6 *Direction for Glide and Circle.*

Glide and Stretch

Tips

* Take care not to hold the sides of your baby as this may tickle when your hands move up their back.
* Remember to lighten the stroke from the buttocks to the ankles so that you are working with the flow of blood in the veins.

Suggested nursery rhyme

Wee Willie Winkie
Runs through the town,
Upstairs and downstairs
In his nightgown.
Rapping at the windows,
Crying through the lock,
'Are the children all in bed?
For it's now eight o'clock.'

Benefits

* Improves posture, muscle tone and general flexibility.

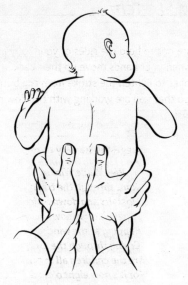

Figure 9.7 *Glide and Stretch hand position.*

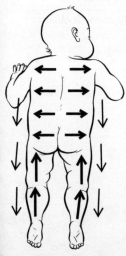

1 Place both your hands flat on the ankles and glide your hands up the legs and over your baby's buttocks.
2 Place your thumbs either side of the spine.
3 Stroke the thumbs out from the spine to the side of the body.
4 Move your hands up slightly after each full stroke out to the side.
5 Continue up to the shoulders.
6 Glide hands back to the ankles (remember to lighten the stroke from the buttocks to the ankles).
7 Repeat three times.

Figure 9.8 *Direction for Glide and Stretch.*

Cat's Paws

Tips

* Use one hand or two, but **do not** put any pressure on the spine.
* Only use the pads of the fingers for this stroke.

Suggested nursery rhyme

I'm only a cat,
And I stay in my place...
Up there on your chair,
On your bed or your face!
I'm only a cat,
And I don't finick much...
I'm happy with cream
And anchovies and such!
I'm only a cat,
And we'll get along fine...
As long as you know
I'm not yours... you're all mine!

Benefits

* Deeply relaxing movement to close the massage.
* Soothes the sensory receptors in the skin.

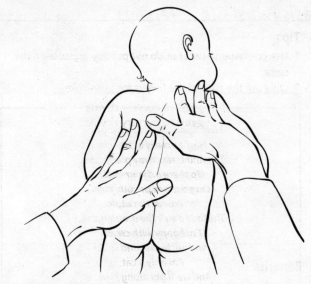

Figure 9.9 *Cat's Paws hand position.*

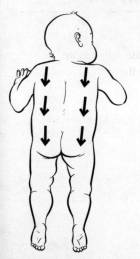

Figure 9.10 *Direction for Cat's Paws.*

1 Use your fingers opened out like a cat's paws (but without the claws!).
2 Stroke from the shoulders down to the buttocks, either side of the spine, using one hand.
3 Repeat with the other hand.
4 Alternate hands three times.

Back Velvet Cloak (again)

Tip

* This stroke signals that the back massage is coming to a close.

Suggested nursery rhyme

Half a pound of tuppenny rice,
Half a pound of treacle.
That's the way the money goes,
Pop! goes the weasel.
Up and down the City road,
In and out the Eagle,
That's the way the money goes,
Pop! goes the weasel.

Benefits

* Soothing and relaxing.

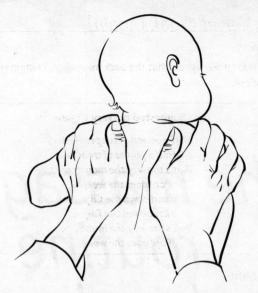

Figure 9.11 *The Back Velvet Cloak hand position.*

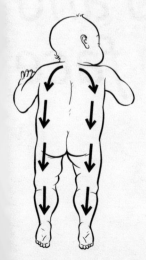

1 Stroke from the shoulders down to the ankles.
2 Remember to lighten the stroke from the buttocks to the ankles.
3 Repeat three times.

Figure 9.12 *Direction for the Back Velvet Cloak.*

the massage routine — head and face

These are the strokes that we advise you to practise with your baby for the fifth week of your massage time together. To ensure that the massage is enjoyable and safe, the massage strokes for the head and face should not be with a fresh application of oil. Take care not to put any pressure on the soft spots on the head.

Once you've asked for the permission of your baby and they have indicated they are happy to have a massage then begin with the Velvet Cloak stroke (see page 31) before starting.

These are the strokes you will cover in this routine:

* Angel Kisses
* Ear Massage
* Forehead Stroke
* Nose and Cheek Stroke

If your baby is happy to continue, follow with the leg, tummy, chest, arm and back strokes that you have already learned at the end. Remember, the new strokes should always come first.

Now you've done a full massage routine. We hope you find time in the future to carry on massaging your baby and having fun together.

Position

* Your baby can be lying on their back or in a sitting position for the head strokes.

Tips

* Remember to ask permission when in Week 5 of the learning programme.
* Remember to do the Velvet Cloak when in Week 5 of the programme.
* Some babies, particularly the younger ones, may resist head and face massage. Introducing them at a later stage, when your baby is used to a regular massage, is always a possibility.
* **Do not apply oil to the head and face.**
* Try to avoid covering your baby's ears during this stroke.
* Take care not to press on the soft spots (fontanelles) on your baby's head.
* When the full massage routine has been learned, we recommend that the head and face is done before the back massage, so that the baby's position is not being changed too often.

Suggested nursery rhyme

Fuzzy Wuzzy was a bear
Fuzzy Wuzzy had no hair
So Fuzzy Wuzzy wasn't Fuzzy
Wuzzy?

Benefits

* Relaxing and calming.

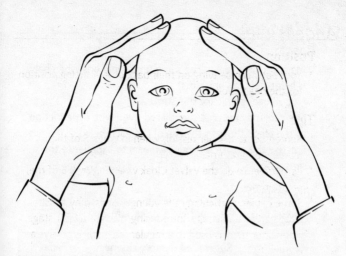

Figure 10.1 *Angel Kisses hand position.*

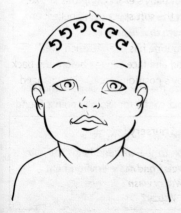

Figure 10.2 *Direction for Angel Kisses.*

1 Using both of your hands, make small circular movements with the pads of the finger tips – cover the whole of your baby's head, ending at their ears.

Ear Massage

Tips

* Massage both ears at the same time (only one when baby is being held in your arms).
* Not all babies will like this stroke.
* The ears may become slightly red, even with little friction, as the blood flows to the rim of the ears (helix).
* Practise this stroke on your own ears to experience the sensation.

Adaptations

* Can be done with your baby in your arms.

Suggested nursery rhyme

Two little eyes to look around,
Two little ears to hear each sound,
One little nose to smell what's sweet,
One little mouth that likes to eat.

Benefits

* This massage will stimulate the auricular points within the ear (and has a similar effect to the reflexology points found on the feet).
* Helps to balance all of the body systems.
* Helps the blood circulation to the ears and helps the baby become more aware of their immediate environment.

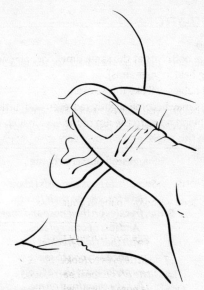

Figure 10.3 *The Ear Massage hand position.*

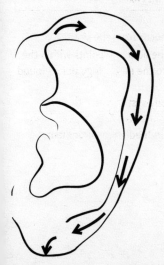

1 Use your thumbs and forefingers and gently rub the rim of your baby's ears (helix) between them, starting at the top.
2 Move down the ears slowly and continue down to the lobe.
3 Now place the pads of your index fingers at the top of the rim of the ears again and in one gentle stroke follow the rim of the ears from the top, round and down to the lobe to soothe the nerve endings.

Figure 10.4 *Direction for the Ear Massage.*

Forehead Stroke

Position

* Lay your baby down on their back for the face strokes.

Tip

* When holding your baby's head, take care not to cover their ears as this can be quite distressing for a young baby.

Suggested nursery rhyme

Some little boys and girls I know
Have freckles on their faces;
Some, freckles on their nose and cheeks
And lots of other places.
I wish that I had freckles too,
For everyone to see.
I wonder what I have to do
To have them land on me...

Benefits

* Can help loosen and drain mucus from the sinuses.

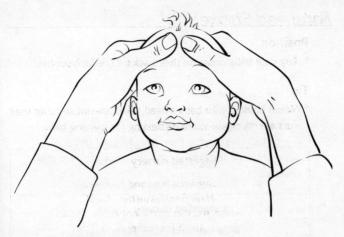

Figure 10.5 *The Forehead Stroke hand position.*

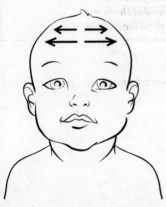

1 Place the flat of the fingers either side of your baby's head, taking care not to cover their ears.

2 Place the flat of your thumbs on the middle of the forehead, above your baby's nose.

3 Gently stroke your thumbs from the centre of the forehead to the temples, above the eyebrows.

4 Repeat three to six times.

Figure 10.6 *Direction for the Forehead Stroke.*

Nose and Cheek Stroke

Tips

* Take care with long nails when stroking down your baby's face.
* Do not cover the ears.
* Not all babies will be comfortable with this stroke. If this is the case, try again at a later stage.
* If your baby is suffering from a snuffle, use this stroke, along with the Toe Rolling (see Chapter 6), to help drain the sinuses.

Suggested nursery rhyme

To be said/sung slowly and quietly.

**There's a Big-Eyed Owl,
With a pointed nose,
Two pointed ears and claws for his toes.
He sits in the tree,
And he looks at you;
He flaps his wings,
And says Toowit-Toowoooo!**

Benefits

* Can help loosen and drain mucus from the sinuses.

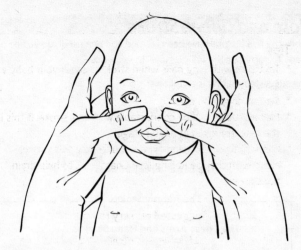

Figure 10.7 *The Nose and Cheek Stroke hand position.*

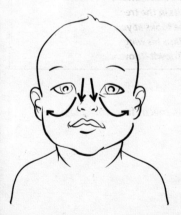

1 Place the flat of your thumbs or the index fingers at the top of the nose.
2 Using gentle pressure, stroke down the sides of the nose and along the bottom of the cheekbones, towards the ears.
3 Repeat three times.

Figure 10.8 *Direction for the Nose and Cheek Stroke.*

The full routine

Once the five lessons have been learned and practised you will be ready to carry out the full massage, in sequence.

The suggested routine is as follows:

Asking Permission
↓
The Velvet Cloak
↓
The Leg and Feet Strokes
↓
The Tummy Stokes
↓
The Chest, Arms and Hand Strokes
↓
The Head, Ear and Face Strokes
↓
The Back Strokes
↓
The Velvet Cloak

Enjoy the massage!